Poetry of Conscious Thought

Volume I

By: T. L. Clause

Dedication

Dedicated to all my family and friends for I have been blessed to appreciate that you are all truly what matters in this life. For gratitude for all my joys.

Remember

Remember to smile each day
A smile is light
Remember to forgive
No one is perfect
Remember to be kind
Kindness is not weakness
Remember to give
Grace can be obtained by giving
Remember to love
That is what life is all about
Remember to pray
God is always your friend.

Forget

Forget nothing
learn from the pain
The past and the present are the tools
towards experience
Experiences should never be forgotten
as they can be the best teacher
Deal with the experiences
Learning not to hold a grudge or
perceive an enemy
Anger controls, stifles your mind
Don't dwell on changing
changes are infinite
Focus on the moment for it is
all that matters.

Friend

A friend is never an inconvenience
A friend can never impose
If either feeling exists, then such is just an
acquaintance.

Touch

I'll hold your hand to touch your heart and
quiet your mind,
You'll understand my love without a word.

A Gift to my Friends

As we go through life, we have many
treasures, or so we think
That house, car, money in the bank
But these are not treasures, just simply
possessions mistakenly thought
to be important
Our own desire for self gratification and
importance
To buy, to have, to control and to own
But I have been lucky enough to realize the
true treasures of life
Love is a treasure
Loyalty is a treasure
Friendship is a treasure
And a true treasure is to find all of those
qualities in one person
A blessing if you find more than one person
To have someone who loves you even on your
worst day
To love someone is when you feel you cannot
give them enough

To hold and share your private thoughts
dreams or secrets without worry that your
weakness revealed will ever become a strike
of consciences
Friendship is life's true treasure surrounded
with all its love and loyalty.

My Angel

An angel appeared last night —
Explain I cannot
Angel Elliot apparently a given name
Graced my dreams
My angel proclaimed
speaking directly to me
Everything would be alright.

Feeling

Feeling as if losing control
Every outward appearance
a routine exercise
Control, brightness and a true leader
obtaining respect from most
Inside, the mind is always fighting those
feelings of doubt
Having everything yet feeling empty
Simply mystified by the realization that
there must be more for purest existence
This cannot be everything
these feelings of nothingness
Searching for purpose
Searching to complete this circle and join
never-endings
In silence, fulfillment is found
These brief moments touched by one's higher
power
Realizing there's more than self
there is neither emptiness nor insanity

On the brink of touching spirit and
becoming one with all
Realizing life eternal and never ending
Giving grace and helping others, true
guidance toward finding purpose.

Independence

Independence of self needlessness, is strength
Being silent and alone is not lonely but
powerful
Falling in love is not a matter of needs
Love is a matter of oneness and sharing
Love will grow and can be independent
Love will change
Love accepts changes and has no fears
Independence embraces love with a sense of
pride and feeling of belonging
Love, a matter of choices.

Act of Silence

Silent
Not because there is nothing to say
Simply because silence is saying something
loudly
Fighting is not worth the aggravation
Know the truth, be loyal
Trust and loyalty
Need no justification
Silence, a comfortable message.

Quiet your Being

Have you ever been too busy?
Too busy to close your eyes?
Too busy to feel,
Too busy to smell,
Too busy to touch,
Too busy to sense what transpires around
you?
Stop, close your eyes, feel that burn
See that candle inside flickering ever so
brightly
Stop — listen to your mind
Listen to your body
Listen to your soul
Quiet your being.

Giving

Pray for guidance to realize what is truly
important
Be a giver, never take
Be a provider to those in need
Need nothing, desire nothing, want nothing
Seek gratification in the grace of giving.

A Fortune

I found a fortune at the end of the rainbow
It makes me laugh, cry and feel beyond
myself
The fortune is my children
I watch in amazement these little ones
Lucky enough to participate in their joys
and successes
A fortune worth more than any worldly gold
Parenthood exceeds any expectations
What a fortune, What a blessing, What a
find!

Words Hurt

Whether planed or not, words can stain the
mind as they touch the heart
Sorry may lead to forgiveness, but ill words
are forever gray
A respect broken by words, words can break
a heart.

Idealization

Idealizations
Giving of heart, soul and mind
Honoring by placing on a pedestal
Love so innocent and true
Life a façade of perfection
Idealization compromised by jealousy, envy,
lack of trust and greed.

Loving Faithfully

Giving the best
Returning respect
Enjoying success
No need to mistrust
Home is with you
Trust is with you
Control and expectations are removed to find
a place of peace
Trust and love without conditions, without
controls
For only at that moment are you truly in
love
Truly loving faithfully.

Loyalty

Loyalty: an honor you give yourself.

Prayer for My Friend

My friend, I pray you are blessed with joy
and contentment
Even when you are alone
To enjoy a moment of silence in an ever so
busy life
To rest after a stressful day with knowledge
that a true friend is your companion
To be kind and giving
To take risks, to love and to be loved
Is my prayer for my friend.

Death is Passing

Death is passing
Overcomes for a moment, as death waits
Death is passing
Death is patience
Death will be another time
Steadily death waits.

Stillness

For a moment there was stillness
Surprisingly there was peace
That lack of sound, that lack of activity
Perfection in the moment
The stillness and silence
Such beauty.

The Dreaming Place

Places of dance are in the dreams
Where suffering has no presence
In dreams reality is challenged
Dreaming, the greatest pleasure
Dreaming, thought cannot control the mind
Dreaming, heart is not in control
In dreaming the mind opens up to the spirit
Encouraging an opportunity.

Heaven's Place

Heaven's place is today
Heaven's place was yesterday
Heaven's place is tomorrow
Heaven's place is infinite existence
Heaven's place is without time
Place is heaven.

Things

Sometimes, things happen
Things have no reason
Things usually don't make sense
Things are part of existence
Things are what they are, when they are,
because they are
Things are extraordinary factors
Things are elements controlled by personal
existence
Things are only part of the existence of now
Things are not a definition of human
existence
Things are growth
Things are learning
Things are development of spirit
Things are ... so
So it must be.

Goodbye

It is hard to say goodbye when someone you
love dies
It is easy to wish you went on that journey
first
Destiny alone controls the termination of
each human existence
Destiny evolving existence
is and will always be eternal
Death, a necessary part of eternity
Death sorrows until eternity is reached
Connections begin to form one
As death becomes nothing, because nothing
ever dies
Because all is never ending and peaceful
bliss.

Angel's Face

I touched an angel's face today,
a precious child's lovely face and both were
comforted by that touch.

Be

Be patient, be kind, be loving be true, be
simple, just be you.

Dream

Give of yourself
More than you have to give
Have no more than you need to feel full
Love more than you dare dream possible
Strive to achieve everything you dream.

No Limits

If the sky is the limit, reach for the next
universe
If impossibility is uttered, make it probable
possibility.

Senseless

Life is senseless
If sensibility doesn't allow for running in the rain, laughing often and playing like a child.

Blessed

If you are blessed to have a child in your life, god is giving you an opportunity to do great things.

Goals

It is your goal, see it, reach for it, achieve it!

Kindness

Be kind, it doesn't hurt anyone.

A Gift to Everyone

Smile, it is great for everyone.

By Chance

By chance we meet
One friend introduced by another
Over time, both becoming friends, and then,
by chance we introduced others.

The Truth

I'll dream tonight of an enchanting place
Where joy will dance and touch the truth.

To Be

Sing to be happy
Sing to live
Sing to smile
Sing to give
Sing to be you.

Present Life

Mindful of the laughter, noise, presence
I smile, I smell, I feel, I touch, lucky to have
so much
Praying, laughing, giving and loving that is
Life!

Searching

When searching for the meaning of life,
search your own heart.

Life's Meaning

Life's meaning is not on far away shores or
purchased at any stores
Life's meaning is in your heart.

Pleasure

Pondering to reach for pleasure, the soul
shall speak
No words are spoken
The touch, the smile, causes awakening of
bliss
Independent, solemn, alone
Enjoying the stillness, of a quiet moment, one
finds pleasure.

Oneness First Draft

There is a place
Such a sacred place
A universally connected space
Which lies dormant in the mind
As consciousness, the born enemy, controls
the pathways of present time
Strengthened by perceptions of Reality
forcing
Thoughts and Truth to hide
Hazed by what was and what will be until
that moment when darkness and light
collide.
As pain and despair make separations heavy
to bear
The truth about the darkness revealed by
unconsciousness, as the luminess lights of all
makes dormant now that mind
With loss of time and place perpetual
vibrations of universally connected lights are
revealed and connected

Breath of forever living tranquility warms
all
As the mind loses its controlling
consciousness the mystery of oneness connects
us all.
As into perpetual existence is sparked by the
loss of what was understood to be knowledge.

The Joy of Nothing

Eyes see only the pictures
Revealed by the heart
Openness of the heart
Floods the heart with love
Floods the heart with lights
Silence comes upon the mind
As the ears hear nothing
Nothing in that moment becomes everything.

New Day

Early morning, majestic time
As a new day is about to begin
Night gives way to sparkles, beams of
sunshine
In this new day's beginning feel the calmness
Cooler air awakens the senses as joined by
the rays of sunshine which warms the space
While your mind's eye is still not completely
focused
Dazed in this calmness, morning's dew on
the ground's cover
What you see is limited.
Close your eyes, listen to nature
Hear the trees roaring; take a deep breath as
the oxygen and sounds awaken your true
being
Thankful and grateful for another new day.

Showers of Sunshine

Showers of warmth, rays of light
Touch the skin
As warmth and body reunite
Showers of Sunshine soften thy being
Moments become filled with the warmth
from the light
Showers of Sunshine
Lying upon the top layers of sands
As the body settles upon
The ground's cool hand
Showers of Sunshine rest upon thy face
As the worlds coolness kisses thy face
Showers of Sunshine, warmth, such grace
Living in stillness this time, this place one
begins to escape
Penetrating warmth with bursts of coolness
opens the pathways
as nature begins to speak.
Noise, wind, the ocean begins to roar, voices
of children eventually disappearing as the
Showers of Sunshine induce deep relaxation

Breathing more deeply
the air so crisp, clean, fresh and salty as the
Showers of Sunshine come to rest.

Tree's Growth

The seed was planted
Would it grow?
Who knows?
Placed with such care as it was given to
Mother Nature
A seed that was planted anchored by roots
showered by Mother Nature's love and care
Then as fate would have overtime
Out of the soil, because of such tools from
light and rain, strong and steady came the
stem
That seed transforms as its roots grow longer
The stem transforms, taller and stronger with
branches and bark
the stem encrusted
entrusted as a living part
Green became such splendor in warmer
summer weather
As the winds began to turn cooler the tree's
green splendor turns orange and yellow with
such fertile fruits for all to see

Cooler and cooler, the bark, it hardens,
shedding the leaves only the branches you
can now see
Winter's snowy white blanket piled on high
Steadier and stronger with the return of
Spring the new season's buds arrive
Now this seed that was planted has become a
strong tree.

Be

Just be
The best be
Friend to be
Wife to be
Mother to be
Daughter to be
Future to be
Harder to be
Just be.

To Achieve is to Believe

Believing in better
Believing in bigger
Believing in dreams
Brings happiness.

Attitude

Attitude is nothing
Positive attitude is everything.

Confidence

Confidence is not arrogant
Confidence is expecting good things by doing
and being good
Honoring oneself and others with one's
positive outlook.

Imagination

Do the right things, make good choices
You know what that is
Truth to honor
Keeping with principles of loving
Keeping with principles of forgiving
Keeping with principles of peace
With these principles, anything wished for is
capable of achievement
Pace yourself as your desires to achieve can
become possessive.
Limitation comes from stalling the
imagination
Opportunities that match imagination with
success
Difference creates a powerful, positive
Failure is of no fault, but it is a whisper to
your promise
Do better next time
Learn from the experience
Triumphant
Doing the best you can do on any given day.

Hope

Living with hope, such a powerful vice
Hoping for the better
Hoping for life
Hoping for happiness
Hoping for confidence
Daring to hope
Hoping for opportunities not yet discovered
Living the big dream, daring yourself.

The Image of Self

Dressing for courage,
that feeling inside
Confidence portrayed outwardly to the
world
Training based on education
or stage in life
Courage in choices
Overwhelming at times
Consuming such confidence portrayed
Weakness, such power
The power of weakness, disguised in fear
that is felt
Energy tapped by the thirst for power
The powerful conquer weakness, conquer
fear and eventually conquer self controlling
the image of confident self
Message to brain
Stop overanalyzing!
Run, analyze, focus and function on
worthiness.

Criticism

Misfortune is criticism failed to be rejected
Accept criticism, it can cause growth
Rejected, criticism condemns
Free thought from blame
Accept all potential — Listen!

Mediocrity

Mediocrity is societal defect
Overcome this obstacle by doing more,
exploring more, learning more being more
than a spectator
Look beyond sight
Beyond self
You believe
Become what you hold as belief
Believe in positive
Toward faithful amazement
As you focus on good
There becomes a spectacular thing.

Boldly

Confidence lacks perfection
Boldly doing what is believed to be true
Achieving more, despite that fact
Perfection conquers its own definition of
successful confidence.

Success

Success is not fulfillment of someone else's
goal
Success is not fulfillment from monetary
tributes
Success accompanied by self persuasion
caused by love
Success creates the great plan toward
happiness.

Desire

Dream to desire
Dream to encourage
Encourage and desire
Live your dreams.

Gift of Word

I give you a gift
Just one word to take on your journey in life
To learn to develop and to grow
The gift of the wind?
"Believe."

.

Unconditional Love

Unconditional love for self
Life's joy shall be bountiful
Love of mind
Love of body
Love of place
Thinking with thoughtful love
Joy shared with others
Rays of love reflections of life
Excitement comes to all contacted
Simplified glowing in unconditional love
and touch
Loving the attitude
Living a good life.

Visualization

Success is visualizing yourself bigger than
what you ever dreamed possible.

Accomplishment

Accomplishment is overcoming insecurities
Everyone has insecurities
Accomplishment revealed from the ability to
handle insecurities.

Actions

Potential all have
Worth from birth
Righteous roars
Endless possibilities
Greatness defined by individuals' actions.

Success in Mistakes

Confidence is allowing yourself to make
mistakes.

Guilt

Guilt
Get over it
Move on
It's useless.

An Angel

Angel trapped
Solitude of condemnation
Realize change
Realize desire
Excellence, performance
An angel is released.

Attitude toward Happiness

Be happy right now, accept this happiness
Any circumstance which existence is present
for happiness
Trust yourself to achieve such happiness.

Progress

Everyday is a new day to work toward
progress
Progress toward being happy.

Possible

Get more than expected
By giving more than you expect
Encounter all expectations and do better
Breeding self worth to overcome obstacles
Conspiring with self for all that is possible.

Joy

Joy is healing
Joy is the potential of a prosperous mind
Joy is simple.

Evil

Evil is your own sense that you are not blessed!

Poverty

Poverty is not materialistic, but a feeling!

Boldness

Boldness with spirituality
Calms your emotions.

Original

Be confident
Never pretend
Be Original, never pretentious
Originality is uniquely important.

Endurance

Individuals have different plans toward
greatness
Common in this plan
Endurance to one's foundation
Individual perfection.

Wisdom

Wisdom is hearing other thoughts in your
decision making process
But following your own heart and sense of
right.

Deception

Deception is deceiving
Deception is negative thinking
Evil taking control
Positive thoughts correct such deception.

Choose

Be great
Choose to let your problems
Strengthen your cheer
Choose to focus your thoughts and attitude
on good things.

Good

Good is Usefulness
Significance in pleasing self.

Pride Worthy

Nobility
Justice
Purity
Virtue
Words are all pride worthy.

Optimism

Be optimistic
Look for good in every person,
Look for good in every situation
Look to self
Look to add
Look to improve
Believing in optimism.

Disobedient

Be disobedient to speculation that is limited.

An Excellent Self

Love is allowing excellence in self.

Trust

Be fearless
Trust in the power of your own greatness.

Direction

Positive thoughts are the proper direction
toward individual strength.

Mind

Calming is a positive frame of mind
Adversity will present itself
Calmly and patiently search for positive
change in the name of mind.

Words Spoken

Words spoken can bring power to life
Words spoken can bring destruction by death
Words spoken can create
Create an environment in words
Words spoken can cure.
Words for healing
Words for happiness
Words for prosperity for all
Words spoken.

Light

A positive atmosphere with encouraging
words can touch all the corners
Turning darkness into light.

Poison

The past is not poison
Just dreams that were not mapped out.

Today

Today, be happy.

Pains

Bury pains of yesterday
Forgive yourself
Emotional health is positive truth.

Toughness

Toughness can be a turning point in your
life
Step into the great future
Believe in yourself.

Overindulgence

Overindulgence corruption of the conscience.

Disappointment

Disappointments are setbacks that form all
new possibilities when focusing
Disappointments are encouragement that
directs your imagination to do better.

Forgive

Forgiveness is letting go for your own best
interest.

Health

Thank you is a healthy word
Giving to oneself, a healthy act.

Wisdom

Wisdom, present in enjoyable times
Observation of family
Observation of strangers
Opportunity, sight giving thanks.

Mind & Heart

Confidence
Positive attitude
Dealing with circumstances
Keep standing
Keeping your mind
A heart true to one's prestigious integrity.

Fairness

Overtone of unfairness
The word of worlds
Encouraging positive attitude
Greets courage.

Spirit

Live honestly
Work and play
Excel in every area of life
Find pride in name and reputation
Actions
Integrity
Promises
Be disciplined
Decisive
Qualities toward spiritual excellence in life.

Make a Difference

Make a difference
Today is all that matters
Yesterday cannot be changed
Tomorrow may not come
Today make a difference
Let those around you know you love them
Let those around you know you care
Greet changes kindly
Greet the world with a smile
Be kind
Speak softly
Laugh
Look for good
Make a difference today.

Breath

Days will be hectic
Breath
Days will be stressful
Close your eyes, breathe slowly
Be silent
Within silence there are answers
Listen to yourself
You're never truly alone
Just listen
Do nothing
Be still
You will experience the energy
Just breath.

See

Close your eyes
Peacefully fall asleep
Resting
Smile
The lights grow brighter
Tranquility becomes you
Gracefully smile
Seconds, minutes, hours, days years
Sociable times
Tabulations of this existence do not matter
Reflexiveness is existence
Close your eyes and see.

Self's Imagination

Sun rises
Night sky
Brilliant kaleidoscope of vibrant colors
Red, yellow, blue the rays, so they shine
I take a breath at the splendor of another
day
A moment
A gift
Feel, See, Smile, Cry, Touch, Be
Self imagination, self's purest gift

Brilliant

Life so brilliant,
Every moment a gift full of joys.

Pure Love

Pure love creates possibilities
Pure love creates hope
Pure love speaks in silence
Eyes reflex, sparks of deep desire
Respect drains knowledge
Joy is a smile
Love is neither servant nor master
Individualism is not fear
There is no guilt in embarrassment
Childish expression without limitation
Life is connected to one's soul and then by
the heart.

Dreams

Miracles of everyday moments
Individuals reaching their goals
Following their dreams
Life not wasted
Listen
Dream
Conviction to times
Tiring
Disappointing
Barely understandable
Fate's sarcastic smile
Desire
Enjoy the journey
The path traveled
The accomplishment along the way
Magic intensifies
Worthy tasks
Daily sacrifice
Surprise full of blessing
Trials and tribulations
Recognizing the conquests

As the moments go by
Against the common
Spirits complete the destiny
Fulfill your dreams.

The Tree

The mind is sometimes foolish
Controlled by sturdy knowledge
Fed by fairies masquerading as greed and
envy
Drunk with expectations
Rehearsed in mannerisms
Proper to a fault
Rooted in traditions of monetary wealth
Brilliant become the branches
That break away from the trunk
Falling from the strong norms
Facing persuasion
Thriving on wisdom based on love and
personal fulfillment
Controlled by the hurt, water to the soul and
cures to society
The approved effects success
Growth of the golden apple of humanity
A gift of giving
Reaching gladness in every moment
Creating and living a dream

The branch seems alive and independent
Stronger then even the physical tree
Dignified by the spirit of joy
Wind, sun and night that flow through the
branch but never inhabit
Promise an obligation to self integrity
Contemplation of tomorrow
Does it ever come, even matter
Realizing the moment in time is still
Scream.

What Happened to Me

At 43 the woman I see,
That woman is unknown to me
The reflection is a woman of achievements
But, what happened to me —
This woman of perfection
What happened to me —
This woman,
A loyal wife,
A loving mother,
A concerned daughter,
A faithful sister
And a good friend
What happened to me —
This woman,
An aggressive professional with a college
degree
Demanding at work,
Punctual,
Refined
Uncompromising
What happened to me?

Monetary goals this woman has achieved
Lost that girlish woman in me
That's what happened to me
I lost simplicity.

Ideal Woman

An ideal woman
An inspiration to all
A private person
Suffering for love
Filling vows unspoken
Keeping private vows
Knowing herself intimately
The mystical being she sees
Lighting the darkness
Words of wisdom
A mother's gift to her child
Acknowledging suffering
Realizing
Teaching that strength that comes from grace.

Compassion

Believing in compassion
Compassion for dreams
Compassion for family
Compassion for friends
Compassion for life
Compassion for God
Compassion for self
Compassion for all people
Compassion for living.

Rose

Suffering is inspiration blooming in the
thorn on the rose.

Believing

Believing is to be
Be kind
Be more
Be faithful
Be loving
Be giving
Be compassionate
Be encouraging
Be enlightened
Be generous
Be silent
Be smiling
Be grateful
Be honest
Be polite
Be friendly
Be true
Be alone
Be a promise
Be simple
Be helpful

Be charitable
Be loyal
Be close to God
Believing in Heaven everywhere on earth
Trust, believe,
Always be listening
Believing.

Motivation

Unmotivated means nothing
In obscurity everything is possible
Importance defined in the little
accomplishments
New day's expressions
Compassion for humanity
Possessed with the gifts to make this world
better
Smaller groups can direct the masses
Toward the importance in making this world
better
Acts of love and compassion motivate and
make everything possible.

Awake

Doubt
Uncertainty
Growth
Growth toward a realization of good
Good for realization of goals
Goals create perpetual pleasure
Perpetual pleasure creates spiritual
awareness.

Darkness

In darkness there is light
Each night, there are stars
Sometimes unseen
No stars
No moon
No clouds
Nothing
Close your eyes
Close your eyes tighter
See the brightness
Shimmering hazes of lights
While the darkest
Search for peace
Look for the shimmering flashes
Joy times three
Peace
Calmness
Openness
Darkness becomes the guide
True lights are seen shimmering.
Hope

Hope the greatest gifts
Hope holds everything
Hope gives everything
Hope is happiness
Hope is Father to the great Divine
Hope is God's secret to humanity
Hope smiles on dreams
Hope fulfills dreams
Dreams create peace
Peace is necessary
Peace is possible if there is Hope
Hope grows into Joy
Hope needs to be taught
Teach Hope
Encourage Hope
Encourage all possibilities
Encourage goodness
Encourage kindness
Encourage family
Everyone can own a piece of hope
Hope is free
Everyone can contribute Hope
Hope is infinite

Lost Hope is shallow, dark and alone
Be Hopeful
Be vigilant for Hope
Be persistent for Hope
Be patient for Hope
Practice Hope
Hope is the true light.

Leader

Inspire a leader
Tell your child daily he or she is loved
Inspire a leader, tell your child daily he or
she is important
Inspire a leader, tell your child daily you
support him or her
Inspire a leader, fill your child's emptiness
with knowledge
Inspire them to listen.
Inspire a leader.

The Secret Right

A secret
Emotions filled by stuff
Thirst of emptiness not quenched
Simplicity is contagious
Enthusiasm requires less
Great love
Smile
Joy
Touch
A kind word
Compassion so questioning
Live with dignity, so when an opportunity
arises for you to do the right you always do
well.

Tears

I sat and wept unconscious tears
Mysterious powers of emotional fears
Not for sadness did the tears fall
Tears caress
Reflections of the past in which
A sense that fate could not escape
A plan for change
Tears of recognition
Tears of unknown
Tears of loss
Tears escape the emotional conscious.

Magical

The world of a dream
The magic
Commitment to dream
Listen to heart's soul
That utmost desire, follow that dream
Sarcastically smiling
Miracles will happen
Following the dream
Disappointment may be experienced
There will be growth
Growth with perseverance reunites the
direction of the dream
Success will be your blessing.

Hectic

Life in the 21st century is filled with vast
non-essentials
Life accompanied with unacceptable
behaviors and attitudes
Hectic has taken over simple
Hectic has taken over practice and patience
Simplistic daily living is neither taught nor
spoken
Focus must be re-directed toward an attitude
of change
From history learn
Future is changed by education
The realization for equality
Realization for Hope
Education of the masses
Classes of Hope
Classes of possibilities and kindness
Goodness, the tool for forging peace
Belief in self
Pride tempered by humiliation
Humiliation relieved by hope

Hope supported by efforts toward
encouragement
Confidant is project strength
Empty is pain and darkness
Laziness that illness that kills the hopeful
spirit
Everyone is important
Everyone has a role
Everyone has possibilities.

Hidden

In the corner of existence
There is a child of tension
In the corner of existence
There is a child unsure
There are all possibilities
Everyone needs reassurance
Checks and balances
Recognized doubts
Listening
Great emotional pains
Balancing
With humility
Life is brilliant.

The Gift

Today is the moment
The gift is joy
Today is the day
Smile
Cry
Give
Love
Live
Today eyes will reveal only human kindness
Love for all mankind
Today is possibilities for hope for all
Today the gift.

Love

Love is silence
Love is joy
Love is a smile
Love is simple
Love has no servitude
Love is guilt free
Love has no fear
Love has no embarrassment
Love is crazy
Love is innocent
Love gives without limitations
Love is childish.

Pledge

Women pledge to be free
Free from guilt
Free from fear
Free from embarrassments of self limitations
Pledge to be strong
Pledge to be confident
Pledge to be loyal
This is a pledge to me.

Sobering

Foolish love so intoxicating
Wisdom from falsely being loved
Foolish thinking of such past controls
Passionate love intoxicating, loyal, unselfish
Love so sobering.

84

Reflections

A glass of wine
Reflection of life
A bottle or more
Life twirled in a sensory reflection of Self
Perception of which changes with each and
every sip
Numbing the brain
Revealing the heart
Spoken strong words
Whispers heard
The conversations
The mood
Mood creates love
The wine opens
Virgin to vanity
Vanity destroys the divinity of self
Impressions of self
Reflected in the glass
The glass empty
Empty is a perception
Reality

Libations
The glass is broken
The wine, no more.

Balance

Life, a committed balancing act
Balancing commitments
Striving to keep "you"
Keeping the abundance of love in your heart.

Defeated

Heartfelt desire a scary commodity
Truth to self powerful energy
Living in light of your grace, the core to
happiness
Defeated applaud your ability to take a
chance
Setbacks essential to your character
Confident in your ability
You worked hard
Excellence is creativity
Vibrant is your success.

Trust

Trust in love
Trust in yourself
Trust in knowledge
Trust in your ability
Trust a successful secret
Calming fears
Encompassing existence.

Forgiveness

Forgiveness is difficult
The mind is slow to forget
Anger is quick, blame is easy
Imperfect humans, fallible and frail
What shortcomings, how imperfect
Virtuous is the grace of the spoken "I'm
sorry"
The masterful art of living kindly
Trusting in good.

Understanding

Everyone has difficulties
Reflecting love in your eyes
Strength from compassion
Taking the path of kindness
Acquiring understanding
Forgiveness by actions.

Daughter

Precious stone
Truest treasure
May your light always shine so brightly
May you know your greatness
Realize your gifts
Reach all your goals
Live all your dreams
Know that you are loved
Love so true
Eternally loyal to your heart's desire.

Eternity

In Eternity I'll meet my friends
In eternity
What a celebration this will be
In eternity
Love, Life, Soul shall be gathered for this
ecstasy
This eternity will be
All loves, family, friends there shall be
Welcome in eternity
Sickness no more, broken hearts healed,
unity without separation
Healed all shall be
In eternity
Connectivity with all souls, home in eternity
No sacrifices, No grief, No tears
Celebration in eternity
With certainty is true, together in eternity.

Son

Confident and loyal
Strong and true
Hard working and kind
Giving and friendly
Understanding and patient
Steady in traditions
A son, such a treasure.

Baby

What a gift this baby shall be
A new life born
Through a painful storm, beauty is born
Voice cries
Love in those little hands
Soft is the skin
Spirit boasts the heart and mind
A baby is born.

Lost Love

Fear is over
Tingling, Numb
Frozen
Silent is the realization of emptiness
Breathe deeply, sigh
Escaping past pretense
Disillusion of Love's faithfulness
Immense pains accompanied
With self's freedom
Over time, stronger and confidant
Fear is over
Love is gone.

Oneness Second Draft

There is a place
Such a sacred place
A universal connectivity space
Which lies dormant to the mind
As conscience the born enemy, controls the
pathways of time
Strengthened by perceptions of thoughts'
reality forcing the truth of what does hide
Hazed by what was and what will be until
that moment when darkness and light
collide
As pain and despair make separations almost
too heavy to fear
The truth about the darkness is revealed by
the unconsciousness
As the luminous light of all makes dormant
now that mind
With such loss of time and place
The perpetual vibrations of universally
connected lights are revealed
The breath of forever

Living tranquility warms all
As the mind loses its controlling conscience
The mystery of oneness connecting us all
As it sparked by the loss of understanding
the limits of mental knowledge.

Husband

Light is brighter by the presence of this man
Glowing is the fire for connection
Desire your body next to mine
Place your arms around my waist
Your lips touching mine
Your scent so memorable
Love so tranquil
Quench all thirst
My dream in this life
Breath so calm
Calms me to sleep
Sweetness is the fountain of this love
Love, Live, Laugh
Learn from each other
My prince charming
Beast
You are my soul, my mind, my heart
All of me, is for all of you
This man I love.

Everything Revealed

My eyes see
Only the pictures
My heart reveals
Only my feelings
Flood my heart
With lights
Silence the mind
Hear nothing
Be nothing
For in this moment of nothing, there is
everything.

Sing

I heard a bird sing
A song of simple sound
I heard a bird sing
Be patient
Be kind
Be true
Be simple
Be you.

Observation

Rooms full of people
Strangers them all
Some tall
Some short
Some fat
Some thin
Some faithful
Some not
Some kind
Some friendly
Some open
Some closed.
Following their own path
Following their dreams.
Some encouraged
Some hopeful
Some bright
Some light
Some angry
Some empty
Some disappointed

Common to all
Seeking a friend
Common whispers make a connection
Exchanges of kind
Observation has changed
Strangers are gone
All seeking a friend, a confidante, a loyal
companion
Most failing to recognize the angel on their
shoulder
Yes, everyone has an angel
A loyal friend
Open the heart
Speak the mind.

Into a Tree

Taller and stronger
With branches and bark
The stem always in the living parts
Green became the splendor in summer's
warmer weather
As the winds began to turn cooler,
Green splendor
Orange and yellow the fertile fruit for all to
enjoy and see
As the weather became cooler, the bark for
all to see
Winter's snowy white weather blanketed
Steadier and stronger with each season's new
buds
A seed that was planted turned.

Believing

BELIEVING IS THE SILENT PART OF BEING,
BELIEVING IS TO BE:
Be Kind, Be Faithful, Be Loving, Be
Compassionate, Be Encouraging, Be
Enlightened, Be Generous, Be Silent, Be
Outspoken, Be Bright, Be Light, Be Smiling,
Be Graceful, Be Honest, Be Polite, Be
Friendly, Be True, Be Loyal, Be Alone, Be
Promising, Be Simple, Be Helpful, Be
Charitable, Be Close to God in all that your
do. *BELIEVING THAT* Heaven is Everywhere!
Trust yourself to always *BELIEVE*, be
Listening for the silent in *BEING* ....

Alive

Early mornings, those majestic mornings
Just as a new day is about to begin
As the night gives way to sparkles of
morning's sunshine
In this new day's beginning
Feel the calmness of being
As the cooler air awakens the senses
You are joined by rays of sunshine slowly
warming the space
While your mind's eye still not completely
focused
In this calmness, with morning's dew
On grounds cover
Close your eyes
Listen to nature's cry
Hear the birds
The trees as nature roars
Take a deep breath
Keep your eyes closed
As the oxygen and sounds awaken your
being

Be thankful
Be grateful for this new day in which you
are alive.

Sunny Day

Showers of Sunshine
Its rays
Its lights
Touch the skin
As warmth and body reunite.
Showers of Sunshine
Soften thy being
Each moment becomes filled with warmth of
the light
Showers of Sunshine
Upon the top layers of sand
Settles the body on the ground
Cool hand
Showers of Sunshine rest upon thy face
As the wind's coolness
Simultaneously kisses thy face.
Showers of Sunshine
Warmth
Such grace
Living in the stillness of time
Begins to escape

The penetrating warmth with bursts of
coolness
Opens the pathways as nature begins to speak
The noise
The wind
The ocean
The roar of the water
The voice of a child
Eventually disappears by the Showers of
Sunshine
Inducing relaxation
Breathing more deeply now
The air
So crisp
Clean
Fresh and salty
With the Showers of Sunshine I come and
rest
Mind Awaken
Mind awaken as Death calls
Body fragile, no fear at all
Mind awaken as Death calls
Windows to thy soul are draped

Suffering begins for those who wait
Mind awaken as Death calls
Soul again reunite seeing never ending
sparkles of light
Mind awaken as Death calls
Cold and darkness greet all
Answered promises are complete spirits'
silhouettes appear
Mind awaken as Death calls
Grieving begins for those who wait
Gathering everyone takes their place
Mind, soul and spirit awaken
Gates of paradise are revealed
Souls and spirits are now one
Mind's job is now done
Uplifting to the lights
With loved ones
All will reunite
Mind is silent
Mind is still
Death is awake
Death is calling.

Grandchild

Your baby boy has grown
How your heart knows his independence
Simple realization that time, once thought to
move so slowly, has passed ever so quickly
You watched with excitement as he crawled,
walked and learned to talk
There were moments, when he talked with
his eyes without ever saying a word
He ran, danced and had an independent
spirit
As his teenage years were tests of wills
However, both survived
As he continuously experienced the world,
Growing from a little boy into a man
Now the time has come
Son is no longer a little boy
A man and a father to be
Your baby boy has grown
Adulthood and parenthood appear to have
been thrusted upon him
A plan you and he foresaw

As your baby boy turned into a man
Yet calm and joyous you become with the
knowledge that a grandmother you will be
Comforting realization another life is born
This grandchild was meant to be
Yes your son has grown and now he is giving
you another part of him to love, your
grandchild, a blessing, a part of your son.

Dependable Friend

Living the good life requires dependable
friends
Dependable friends make the celebrations
and life complete
Dependable friends contribute to happiness
Dependable friends become part of our select
group of individuals called family
This good life given by choice not birth right
Dependable friends share in our joys and
cheer
Cheering the successes in life
Dependable friends are steadfast
When the troubles of life unexpectedly drop
by for a visit
Dependable friends are constant
Dependable friends are thoughtful
Dependable friends are loyal
Dependable friends are honest but kind
Dependable friends just happen
Dependable friends are gifts

Coming into our lives just at the right
moment
Dependable friends fill a tremendous void
Dependable friends are the people you could
not, imagine your life without
Dependable friend sees through your words,
sees your insecurities and supporting you
silently
Dependable friends are not time consuming
and needy
Dependable friends just stop by to visit
Dependable friends forgive your
imperfections
Time with dependable friends passes swiftly
Suddenly you're 49, almost 50
Dependable friends are an indispensible
part of living a happy life
Dependable friends are true treasures.

Good Day

Breathe
Today shall be a good day
Wake, wash, and dress for today
Pause, breath, prepare your appearance of
outward strength
Remind yourself
Today shall be a good day
Decide to love yourself
Decide to love those you meet
Act as though today is a good day
Be strong physically, fighting off any
emotional insecurities
Fighting the battle
Today is a good day
Cry if you must, but cry alone
Then take a moment
Smile on
Today is a good day.

Alone

The hustle and bustle
Busy but alone
The dark is darker
When alone
Confused
Gain control
No one is ever alone.

Symmetry

Women are different from men, no doubt
The obvious physical differences are
apparent to see
The softness of the woman's skin, the
fragrance of her hair
Compared to the chiseled jaw of the man
and his crew cut hair
Visible differences no doubt
But truth be told, woman and men are more
alike than the eyes can see
The ying and the yang of similarity
Woman bleed, Men bleed
Woman cry, Men cry
Woman love, Men love
Women share, Men share
Woman shine, Men shine
Woman care, Men care

Woman have fears, Men have fears
Emotional similarities are without a doubt
The symmetry of woman and men is love
Because without love, both are miserable
and of that there can be no doubt.

Solitude

Contemplating nothing
Leads to magnificent solitude
Hearing the air, the echoes of voices
The crackling of heating systems turning on
and off,
The cars rushing by, the papers turning, the
wind
Seeing a room void of people yet full of life,
the lights,
The moth that twirls in the air,
The flag that moves from the wind blowing
in from the single pane window,
The chairs,
The desks,
The benches full of history prepared for the
future
A calmness that is soothing
Emptiness that engulfs your presence as you
become part of the events.
Feeling the warmth of the light,
The freshness of the air

Smelling the environment
Touching your being
A moment of nothing
How fulfilling simply nothing can be
Simply alone
As the second hand turn on the clock
Contemplating time as it moves
Sixty seconds
Maybe more
The topic is nothing.

Making the day Special

Today is the day
Today is special
Today hug your family
Today call a friend
Today say hello
Greeting a stranger with a smile
Today appreciate a job well done
Today strengthen the environment with
positive passion for all people
Today pray
Today be thankful
Gratitude makes today special

Thank You

Today began just like another day until I
realized that today is a new day
Until I realized today is the only day that
matters
So today, I realized to love more and give
more
Today I realized to question why
Because today is all this is
Today is all that matters.

True Commitment

A commitment
Separate and distinct
United as one
Sharing love, joy, family and friendship
Soul mates bound by the blessing from God
Promises of respect,
Promises of kindness
Promises of forgiveness
Honoring each other with tenderness and
loyalty
Creating dreams
Memories for eternity
Separate individuals now united,
A Powerful onion of one
One union that will persevere through time
One union growing deeply in love with each
other
A union that honors life's true commitment.

Listen

Angels know
they listen
They let you go
God is always ready
A place always prepared
All eventually will be there
Joy is never ending
Love everlasting
Angels provide for family here on earth and
in Heaven
Blessing pass with prayers
Grace cares of others
Alone you will never be, for
Greatness is foreseen.
A kingdom awaits.

The Lineage of Friendship

The lineage of friendship starts with a word
A simple word, "hello"
At that initial exchange, words create
possibilities for the growth of friendship.
The lineage of friendship has begun
Like the great tree of life the "Baobab Trees,
this beginning starts with something simple,
a seed
The friendship evolves with celebrations,
cups of tea, martinis and dinner parties.
Spending time together
Acts of kindness help the friendship grow
Friends encourage dreams
Friends are sympathetic to worries
The lineage of friendship evolves with
celebrations, like the Baobab Trees' seed
grows into a trunk with branches and leaves,
Sturdy and strong
The lineage of friendship forms a bond
Friendship that is bound with faith
Friendship bound with trust

Friendship bound with honesty
Friendship's bond, sealed with loyalty
The lineage of friendship, as the "Baobab"
Tree bark can be resistant to any attack by
fire
Scoff at the driest droughts
Creating one of the world's largest living trees
The lineage of friendship a strong covenant
Resistant to any attacks by strangers
As friendship becomes strong
Fruitful
Endeavoring all the tragedies of life
Creating cherished memories
The friendship, the trunk from this lineage
of friendship heals emptiness
The lineage of friendship is enjoyed
Supported with helping hands
The lineage of friendship promotes calls just
to say hello
Immeasurable is the value of the lineage of
friendship

Friendship the joy of living.
The lineage of friendship is infinite
happiness.

Love's True Commitment

That special day
Your Wedding Day
Both of you professing your love for each
other
A ceremony in front of God, family and
friends
All hearts are filled with an abundance of
joy
All hearts are filled with enthusiastic
happiness
All hearts and minds are filled with pure
love
All in attendance in Heaven and on Earth
will wish you both a lifetime of
togetherness
The delight of the moment will be
overwhelming
That feeling of True love ever so bright
Two lives of living are now one
Life's everyday journey will encompass your
life

Playing a tug-of-war with your united
spark
That candle's light ,True Love
Commitments to others become a daily tug-
of-war
Your strength is this True Love
Struggles for balance frustrating
Your Special Wedding Day
Sometimes that love on that special day will
seem so far away
Have faith
True Love is always steadfast
True love is patient
True love is persevering
True Love burns bright in your hearts
Stop and listen to your Heart
Easy it shall be to honor this union of love
with respect for each other
Easy it shall be to honor this union of love
with trust for each other
Easy it shall be to honor this union of love
with time spent with each other
Hold true to your commitment

126

A commitment to be kind to each other
A commitment to listen to each other,
A commitment to work together and disagree
politely
A commitment to say your sorry and to
forgive
A commitment to speak to each other about
pains and goals
A commitment to Work Together to enjoy
simple pleasures of life
A commitment to laugh
A commitment to love
A commitment to have fun together, even
when money is tight and things go wrong
This is a commitment to TRUE LOVE.

Millennium

May you be blessed with good health,
unconditional love and unparalleled
happiness for the millennium, for your life.
Incandescing mind at peace with yourself,
your family, your friends, your goals, your
God, and
YOUR LIFE
Laughter that is well intended and
simplified fun which harms no other, but
makes you capable of recalling the past and
occasionally living, learning and laughing
at yourself and
YOUR LIFE
Life, that is long and filled with memories of
good food, good friends and good living,
which encompasses
YOUR LIFE
Ever blooming bounty of prosperity in your
work, your home and
YOUR LIFE

Nourishment that comes from intellectual exchanges of values and ideals with respect and understanding of those positions in which you disagree in YOUR LIFE
Noteworthy acts of anonymous gratitude and kindness, done by yourself and others in
YOUR LIFE
Isolation which is solemn that makes you contemplate the meaning and purpose of
YOUR LIFE
Unassuming persona that is balanced, uncanny, respectable and forgiving, in the life of others and
YOUR LIFE
Magnanimous spirit, mind and body that exudes in every act, of every minute of every day of the rest of your life, and the lies of those you touch as you go through
YOUR LIFE.

Legacy of Faith

No records of wrongs
No self seeking prowess
Reflections of love
Guilt abandoned
Legacy of faith
Forgiveness released
Golden values of love and kindness for the
world, family, and friends
Trust, hope and perseverance
In the future you will fail
In failure learn
Get hurt, get over it
Kind words
Encouragement
Compassion for all toward suffering no more
The chance to forgive and be forgiven
The legacy of faith.

Aversion

Adversity absolutely predictable
Responses to adversity
Development of character
Life's roles
Life's responsibilities
Respond thoughtfully
Respond meticulously.

Potential

A treasure
Hidden self
Parent
Diligent worker
Loyal friend and companion
Self-reliant
Heart felt existence
Questioning the relationship to oneself
Daring to believe
Personal greatness is possible
Graciously facing challenges
Unexpected friendships with crushing
frankness
Probably no one expected much
Particularly self
But the unexpected came to BE
A treasure of accomplishments achieved
A daughter who is an artist and loving adult
A son who is witty and an adventurous
adult
Supportive family.

Congratulations

Pearls, Diamonds, Gold and Rubies are a
few momentary treasures
Treasures found in the sparks of valuable
jewels
Jewels that can be locked in a safe
Owned by the wealthy few
Common jewels exist despite society's
pressures
Common jewels that are more valuable than
monetary treasures
Jewels Gifted at birth
Jewels inherited by right
Silence yet shouting
Calm and fearless
That welcomed a sparkling smile,
Kind greetings
The act of giving
So simple
Common jewels for valuable living.

Hidden Pictures

Picture of perfection
Emotional inferiority
Feelings of insufficient self worth
Confident face hides feelings of doubt
Emotional balance
Appearance of assurance
Great compassion without vulnerability
Picture perfection.

Grateful

Life begins
Hear soul's thoughts
Time passes
Every minutes a gift
Gratefulness every day
Tender moments
Moments shared
Calmness
Storms
Knowing
Unknowing
There is more
There is less
Facing the truth
Not being afraid
Facing the present
A reflection
Grateful

Warmth

Scrutinizing
The image of self
Unaware of exactly who I am
Searching for answers
An elusive task
Success equates to more questions
Answers hidden by the depth of worldly
persuasion
Self shadowed by appearances of comfort
Livelihood is strengthened
Cherished moments of alone
Cherished moments of silence
Unspoken responsibilities
Obligations
Soul begins when the silence is heard
Coherent self is attained
Self un-chaperoned in silence
Authority to be

Pure existence of being intoxicated by fierce
sentiments of pure existence of love, of light
Pure existence of beginning
Warmth compassionate to one's reflections.

Encouragement

Encourage yourself to do more
eat
work
sleep
Believe in your dreams,
Commitment to happiness
Bigger dreams
Future happiness
Each day give a little bit more of yourself
Your actions
Your words
Take a deep breath
Love
Echoes of hurt
Tears
Help with a smile
Words of encouragement

A soft touch
Let your life sing
Let your life dance
Sleep, with an open window to
encouragement.

Tingling

Driving I felt the tingling touch
Combing my daughter's hair, I felt the tingly
touch
Encouraging my son, I felt the tingly touch
Quiet moments sleeping next to my husband,
I felt the tingly touch
In church I felt the tingly touch
The tingling touch of love.

The Fellowship of Family

A baby is coming, what a wonderful joy!
The baby is a precious thing
A blessing sent from Heaven above
A treasure to the special couple
Forever a family
Individuals will transcend into parents.
Lives will never again be separate or the
same.
Embark upon this journey with open minds
and hearts
Neither a Degree nor predetermined
qualifications need be
This journey into parenthood holds INFINITE
possibilities of love
This love for each other immense, but
immeasurable compared to the love for this
child
Never-ending love for your child
Your souls united in the Cosmic Universe
forever as one
Long is the journey

There will be times you will question your
skills
Times you question your decisions
Parents united as one
One as Mother, the other as Father
Moments will be overwhelming,
Time will move ever so quickly
Love deepens
Intrinsic desires to experience the purest love
Kindness
Warmth
Overcoming uncertainties that you will face
as new parents
Welcoming your new baby
The baby smiles,
You hear the laughter,
Tears will fall
Disappointments and triumphs part of your
journey
The privileged passage of the benevolent
transformation from individuals into the
REALM OF PARENTHOOD

Parenthood intertwining individual essence
of being into the united fellowship of
FAMILY
Family unity in love
Blessed by grace
Family the true treasure.

Succeed

Blunt frankness
Abundant blessings
Unexpected twists of fate
Career which was thought only as a Dream
Dreams began to be possible
Wisdom obtained
Life's dream spent with family, friends
Displaying love
Tedious nights
Studying
Doubts
Dreams can be difficult
Imagine achieving
Failure exposing self
Times of anger
Times of frustration
Times of anxiety
Another speeding ticket
Giving up
Harbored feeling of impossibility
Perseverance

Growth
Maturity to reach the power in life
Quiet guidance
A childhood brightly lit the path to succeed
Recognize all possibilities
Accomplishments
Educational degrees
Hard work
Self reflection
The image is stronger
Living your dreams
Expecting the unexpected while living a
dream.

Observer

Sit quietly
Listen
You can hear so much
Quietly breathe
Become part of your environment
Realize the smells
Realize the air
Realize the people
Realize the places
Be an observer
Learn so much more.

To Be Opposed Upon

A friend is someone
who can be imposed upon
Everybody else is an acquaintance.

Achievement

Give more
More than you have
Have no more than you need
Love more than you can dream
Dream more than you can achieve
Achieve everything.

Me

Every family member holds a special place
for a kindred heart
Mother, father, brother, sister, family
Learning love
Learning faith
Learning kindness
Challenged by hurt
Patience, envy, and desire
Souls searching
Family encompassing expanding to include
friends, husband, sons, daughters daily
acquaintances, all extended family members
Quenching desires for fullness
searching for me
Souls reflect on past, souls reflect on present,
and souls reflect on future
Difficult times transcend into growth,
Building strength
A Souls' perseverance amend negative
experiences
Richer

Fuller
Complete
Kindness
Love
Souls ponder positive impacts of Giving
Present reflections of "me" of "them"
Search for the future
Desire to reach fullness
The wholeness of "all"
The answer
The past
The present
The future
Family
Experiences
Worldly assets cannot quench
Quench the desire to be
To reconnect to all
To be all of me
Quenching souls
Only over time
"Me" was found in love
"Me" was found in a smile

"Me" was found in patience
"Me" was found in kindness
"Me" was found in giving
"Me" was found in forgiving
giving up I
Physical "me"
Spiritual connected to all.

Happiness

Happiness is self evident
Happiness is about self
Happiness is about "I"
Happiness is reached for by everyone
At some point in life (truth be told) achieved
by few
Happiness is simply
Decide to be happy
Full of grace for myself
Happiness is "I" inspirational
"I" loved
Happiness is found within.
Personality is potent rival
Personality which is worthy
Personality an ambitious revolutionary
Personality dominating

Intellectual
Sophisticated
Personality can be imprisoning
Capturing your greatness
Let happiness consume
Your ego become your happiness.

Treasure Box

It takes a Lifetime for some to realize Living
is the true treasure
Living is not about the house you own, the
car you drive or the money in the bank
Living is simple
Living is the everyday miracles
Following your dreams is Life's Miracle
Living is being true to you, but at the same
time, kind to others
Living is the everyday acts and words of
kindness that you give and receive.
Living is giving of yourself more than what
is expected in all that you do
Living is taking only what you need and
sharing with others

Living is making mistakes.
Living is learning from your mistakes
Living is having quiet time for you
Living is the children, friends and family
Living is learning to love yourself
Life is living with LOVE
Love is LIFE.

Goals

If the sky is the limit, then reach the next
universe
If impossible is uttered, make it possible
If probable is a possibility, then make that a
goal.

Sensibility

Life is senseless if sensibility doesn't allow
for running in the rain, laughing often and
playing like a child.

Greatness

You are blessed to have a child in your Life.
The child is giving you the opportunity to do
great things

Love is not Perfect

Love is living with silence when words
would hurt
Love is a resting place from the pretense of
our persona
Love is watching each other grow
independent, but having a lot to share
Love is giving generously.
Love is liking each other even when you
realize that each is not perfect
Love is perfect!

Reflections of Kindness

Reflections of kindness
That doesn't hurt anyone
A Smile
Great for everyone, a smile.

Absolutely

Absolutely should be a course
Taken as a positive source
Learn to say yes
Try new things
Refreshing this adventure can be
Satisfying and fun
Absolutely, of course.

A Note

At your darkest moment
Do not be afraid
You are lucky
Be there in that moment
Touch your heart
Healing from pain
Brighten your thoughts
Weakness revealed
Dark shadows, movement
Eternal lights
Love, only a whisper away.

A Whisper from Your Soul

Most hear but do not listen
Most touch but do not feel
Most see but do not have insight
Few leave their minds
Forgoing that game of reason
Enhance your inner feeling
Enhance your heart's beating
Experience emotions
Positive and negative emotions
Just experience it all
Strive for a balance
Unify the mind with your heart
Follow those whispers
Hopeful, loving whispers
Shhhh ....

My friend

I declare boldly admiration my chosen
friend
Our strong connection
Give rise to victory
Words and moments
Confirming pure truth
Life is good
Life is eternal
My friend good
Trust
Good attracts good
Kindness
Leaps of faith
Joy of friendship
Healing a fusion
Mighty friends
Soldiers of light
Indistinguishable
Steadfast
Supporter of unspoken dreams
Calming

Witnessed miracles
Witnessed mirages
Laughter my friend
Glanced cautiously into each other's souls
Loyal is my friend
We are power
Graced with supporting each other's dreams
Encouraging positive outcomes
Magnitudes of obstacles
Reflecting deeply in spirituality my friend
Bound by conscious decision of joy and
happiness
The creation of friendship
Prosperity money cannot buy
My friend
A mirror helps see
True reflections of dreams
Imagination
Companionship
My loving friend
Consciously dwelling in wishes
Happiness independent friend
Ignoring malfunction

Trusting
Healing
Loving
Victory
Certain
You are my friend.

Beautiful Green

Starting out as part of one
Clinging to sturdy branches for existence
Independent, one grows
Stretches to encompass a miraculous seasonal
sight
Foundation seeds makes one union with
another
As the foundation grows and develops
The seeds fall
The seeds grow
The seeds become part of one
Marvelous a sight of strength
Endurance and life
Each year that passes
Changes occur
The seedling grows
Reached out to the world

The start of one ages
Weathering with passing time
A beautiful sight
Ever changing with each season
Beautiful is this tree.

Common Beauty

Beauty is common
Beauty in everyday moments
The sun rises, beauty beams into the window
The sun sets beauty shines in the night
The stars shine lighting the evening path
Everyday routines
Parts of daily life
That first cup of coffee
Touch
Smells
Feelings of grace
That kiss goodnight
"I love you" husband
"I love you" daughter
"I love you" son
'I love you" mother
"I love you father, sister And brother
"I love you friend
"I love you" self
Love is what matters
Smile greets a friend or stranger

Beauty is common
Beauty is all around
Beauty is learning to live
Adventures engaging in life
Emerging self with beauty
Eloquent happiness, existence in such beauty
Realizing the essentials of life surrounded
by beautiful living
Beauty in the everyday
Beauty in breathing
Beauty is Grace
Living for the moment.

Restful Mind

Tired
It's time to rest
There are always things to do
Race, race, stop this hectic pace
Commitments
Obligations
Responsibilities are never ending
Mind needs to stop
Take time to rest
Listen to your body
Quietness
Peace
Solitude
Mind at rest
Everything will all be all right
Mind at rest
Mind goes to sleep, mind at rest
Mind however controls one's rest.

Choices

Right versus wrong
Good vs evil
Every choice a consequence
Make the right choice
Make the good choice
Make wrong choice
Make evil choice
All impossible to eliminate
All positive choices impossible
All negative choices impossible
Possibility to learn from all those choices
Balancing hope
More good than evil
More right than wrong
Choices are all the possibilities.

Soul's Birth

Every soul has an inauguration into
physical existence
birth
From the moment of birth, the soul's
physical and mental existence develops
Unfolding from emotionless, simplistic
To a mindful spiritual soul of existence
Struggling with the complex calibration of
reasoning and knowledge
Searching for developments which
illuminated the soul
Illumination which is a constant peaceful
existence
Illumination returning to an emotional
pleasure
Simple existence in the present.

Pledge to Children

Pledge to my children
Give attention
All that is needed and desired
Listen attentively
Sometimes, silence is speaking
Smile encouragingly
Give unselfishly
Love unconditionally
Teach politeness
Independence
Family values
Support all wins
Understand the losses
Emotional ups and downs
Kindness
Humility
To teach generosity
Be patient
Kiss and hug
Loving shall be a priority in life
Recognize good friends

Learn to deal with challenging individuals
Love, love yourself, love others
Have fun, laugh, smile.

Clouds

Gray clouds will disappear
Light can always be found
Stop, listen to the silence
Humanity is speaking
Feel the sun
It exists always
In any storm, under any condition
Close your eyes
Silently wait to feel the sun
Kindness is a smile
Goodwill is a positive word
Positive possibilities
Being critical is not courageous
Courage is being silent
Courage is being kind
Courage is being comforting
Courage is explaining
Living without love is lifeless
Living without family is lifeless
Living without friends is lifeless
Living without God is lifeless

After death there is life
The sun always shines
Open your heart
Feel the sun.

Possessions

Possessions are weapons to human suffering
Possessions are weapons to human desire
Possessions are weapons to human need
Possessions are weapons to human greed
Possessions are weapons to human
superiority
Held at bay by love
Held at bay by family
Held at bay by friends
Held at bay by God
Spirited acts of caring
Spirited by act of sharing
Spirited by acts of honoring
Spirited by acts of respecting
Spirited by acts of giving
Spirited by acts of believing
Spirited by acts of praying
Spirited by acts of loving
Touch, so healing.

Touch of Prosperous Love

Words of heart unspoken
Announced in what is observed
Felt in what is inherent
Blessed with acts of love
Blessed with acts of respect
Blessed with support
Inspired by encouragement
Positive motivations
Future is family
Family touched and loved
The power of family encompasses all dreams
The power of family encompasses happiness
Revealing successful living
Belonging
Connected
Touching heightens love
Love a tremendous blessing
Opportunity for unconditional happiness
Neither critical not harsh
Neither discouraging nor distending
Neither insecure, nor interfering

A harp playing kindness
Compassion embraced in acts of love
Encouraging dreams
Achieving greatness
A touch of prosperous love.

Everything is Possible

A child
Dreams embraced in imagination
Anything thought possible
Innocent optimism inherent in thought
To dream to live
A child
Incapable of pessimism
Pessimistic thoughts are taught.
A child grows with age its adolescent years
Those adolescent experiences changes a child
physically and emotionally
An adult
Love, encouragement and dreams.
An adult
Embraces imagination
Everything is possible
Following your dreams
Everything is possible
Surrounded with optimistic people
Believe in yourself
Loving yourself

Everything is possible
Loving your family
Everything is possible
Work toward goals
Fulfill your dreams
Learn from every experience
Nothing is ever wasted
An adult, following dreams, embracing
imagination
Become a successful person
An adult who has achieved
Because everything was possible.

Motherhood

Becoming pregnant
Becoming a mother
Experiencing ranges of emotions
Joy
Bewilderment
Contentment
Unease
Frustration as the body rearranges
Expanding a humble Mother-To-Be
Encompassing her every thoughts, this child
soon for her to see
An enigmatic mental belief
Desire that she is going to be a Perfect
Mother
Struggling with the realization that as a
Mother-To-Be she has no idea what
perfection is or how this concept of perfection
will evolve her
Reality this new lifetime journey
Commitment to Motherhood it shall be

Neither books nor other mothers' experiences
will quench the yearning for knowledge
Becoming a Perfect Mother it shall be.
Uneasy realization there is no predetermined
amount of knowledge attainable
To reach this goal
A Perfect Mother
Satisfaction mentally doubtful, no perfect
shall there be.
Role as mother forever changing
Connecting mother and child without a
degree
Your own experiences as a mother, to your
child, will become your knowledge
Desire for perfection
Acts of respect, acts of love, acts of
commitment
A mother's gift to her child
Your spirit fulfilled
With the blessing of your child.

A Friend

There are people we meet in life
People who become familiar
There are people we are born with in life
Genetic relationships
Then there are people you can consider
friends
True friends will know your secrets and
never share them with anyone.
True friends will always be there for you,
even when you have been difficult and
unreasonable
True friends are people you laugh with, cry
with, and enjoy even silence with
True friends are patient and understanding
True friends will not always agree, but will
always be respectful
True friends give unconditionally their love
and heart
True friends are people you escape with over
a cup of coffee

True friends can catch up on a relationship
without missing a beat
True friends know when to speak and when
to be silent
True friends know when you're drowning
physically and mentally quickly throwing
you a lifeline
True friends are spiritually equal
True friends don't need to call daily but
thinks of your friendship daily
True friends are honest, but kind
True friends can sense uneasiness
True friends are loyal.
True friends enjoy each other's company, no
matter what you're doing
True friends are supportive
True friends understand compromise
True friends knows your obligations
True friends can see through your persona
when no one else can, seeing your true
existence
True friends are the greatest treasure.

Promise

A promise is a gift
Of integrity
A promise is a gift
Of words
A promise is a gift
Of meaning
A promise is a gift
From the soul
A promise is one of the most valuable gifts
Bestowed with the honor on its recipient
A promise —
Honest, heartfelt, and simple
A promise has only one meaning
To be true
A promise
A reflection of
the promissor's persona
A promise
A gift
A promise is truth.

If Death Comes Today

If death comes today, it shall be sad
Children shall be missed
Companions shall be missed
Parents shall be missed
Friends and family shall be missed
Souls shall be at peace
God is always close at heart
The spirit an extension
Laughter forever shall be
Smiling hearts in heaven
Grace provides guidance each day
Meetings occur
Comfort touches your face
Comfort graces your body with warmth
Hearts will beat
Whispers from the past
Guidance descends from above
Angels blessing
Living energy surrounds all
Death vanishes.

Gifts to my Children

Presented to you
The most valuable gifts
Anything in this world
What shall I gift?
The gift of a smile
To brighten each day
The gift of perseverance
To have the ability to try and try again
until you get it right and succeed
The gift to follow your dreams
Dreams that will guide your heart to
fulfillment
The gift of simplicity
To make your life simple
To enjoy sun
To enjoy the rain
To enjoy the moon
To enjoy the stars
To enjoy the snow
The gift of literacy to read and educate

The gift of giving generously
The gift of forgiveness
To let go and say you're sorry
The gift of love
The gift to enjoy good friends, family and
your God
The gift of prayer, to learn to communicate
with yourself and your higher power
The gift of quiet and solitude, to find you
The gift of kindness, to serve others and
yourself
The gift of loyalty
The gift to honor your words,
your promises
The fortitude to tell the truth
The gift to love,
to allow someone to share your life
These are my gifts, which I bestow upon you.

A Promise to Self

Promise to be me
Promise to be honest and true
Promise to share good days and bad day
Promise to sing
Promise to laugh
Promise to cry
Promise to agree and disagree
Promise to love
Promise to talk, even when talking is
difficult
Promise moodiness sometimes
Promise to love
Promise to have fun and on occasion, be sexy
Promise to worship
Promise to be thankful
Promise, that children come first
Promise to make a house a home
Promise to enjoy life
Promise to be kind
Promise sometimes there will be anger
Promise to never break a promise

Promise to love yourself always.
End of the Day
At the end of each day
Thank God for blessings bestowed upon life
Thank God for husbands hardworking and
loyal
Thank God for sons and daughters
Thank God for family and friends for
without either life would be empty
Thank God for work and the ability to
provide comforts
Thank God for all the challenges throughout
the day
For without challenges, life would be boring
Thank God for another day in allowing the
enjoyment of sun and rain
Thank God at the end of each day.

Life

It is not about what we see
It is not about what we think
It is all about feelings
Self's feelings
Others' feelings
Feelings of the beginning
Being true to Self
Being faithful to one's own truth
Being connected by others
Appreciating now
Appreciating the present moment
Realizing what was has passed
Realizing what is current is all that matters.

Today I Shall Be

Today is here
Therefore, I will be
Fullness shall be part of my heart
The sun
The moon
The stars
The beginning
The end
All shall be
Troubles
Friends,
Family, with focus I shall be
Today, I shall pray
Thankful for living another day
Today I shall be all that I can be
Today I shall touch all that I can touch
Today I shall be
Today I shall love as much as I can love
Today I shall be
Today I shall sing
Today I shall dance

Today I shall walk
Today I shall run
Today I shall work
Today I shall play
Today I shall be
Today I shall learn
Today I shall give
Today I shall receive
Today I shall be
Today I shall hurt
Today I shall heal
Today I shall feel the pain
Today I shall feel joy
Today I shall be
Today I'll pursue
Today I'll reflect
Today I shall be
Today I shall be ME.

The Flame

Mind's flame sparked
By knowledge
Mind's flame fueled
By desire
Mind's flame in light
By family
Mind's flame
Eternal by love.

The Soul

The truth
The light
The promise
The comfort
The constant
The good
The forever
The now
Talking to Being
Being one with all that is bright
A smile
A laugh
A glow
Hope, one with brightness
Hopeful being.

The Darkness

The coldness as day's end
Greets darkness with stillness
Darker and Darker turns each hour until
midnight's hour
That hour
That moment
The cold
The dark
The Stillness
Joined by shouting silence
This silence
This sanctuary
Dreaming for yet another day
Fears
Angers and doubts
The now becomes unbearable
An instant
In the darkness
The coldness
The escape
Forever still.

Legacy of Words

These are the words which meanings I lived by each day. My legacy of words.

1.   Love – Its power euphoric. Love yourself, love your God, Love your family, Love your friends, Love strangers. Love your enemies, Love your job, Love each day, Love your life.

2.   Kindness – Show kindness always, be good, do good, be considerate, be silent, speak softly.

3.   Honesty – To yourself, to your reflections, to others in all you do tempered with kindness.

4.   Charity – Learn to give of yourself, give of your time, give your assets to all worthy causes. You do not need to give publicly, but quietly by acts of giving your rewards will be unending.

5.   Integrity – Be true to yourself, your life, your word. Be a person you would trust.

6.　Knowledge - Learn something new each day. Read, write, teach and learn. Knowledge is power.

7.　Compassion – To forgive yourself, to forgive others. To understand and try again. To be a gracious winner and even a more gracious loser. To learn every lesson is an experience toward self growth, nothing is ever wasted.

8.　Humility – to laugh at oneself, to cry, to scream, to walk before you run.

9.　Belief – Believe in yourself. You're important, you're great, there are no limitations, no impossibilities. Everything is just possibilities.

10.　Grace – non judgmental, silence toward a tranquil state of unconsciousness.

11.　Spirituality – Positive sense of well-being, connections to a greater energy.

12.　Holiness – Connecting with your higher power.

13.　Oneness – Your connection of energy to all that is and will be.

14.   Solitude – The ability to reflect, to think, to ponder, to be silent and alone without fear.

15.   Manners – This is simple. The basic courtesies. Please, thank you, your welcome and a smile.

Awake

Awaken early
Soft lights, sun off in the distance
Darkness slips away
Red turns to orange
Orange to yellow
Such bright shiny warmth
A new day
A beginning, another chance
For this day, all that matters
To be
To listen
To speak
To be present today
All day, all that matters
Reflections of vivid dreams, all that matters
Gifted wisdom
On what matters
Staying young at heart and mind
Enthusiasm for every day
Think with your mind
Be conscience

Travel to new places
Do new things
Visit the old
Take time to be alone
Appreciate what you have
Teach others, for today you are all that
matters.

Mankind

Follow your dreams and imagination.
Believe in yourself and mankind.
Every day smile, be kind, perform a random
act of good and call home.
Living a happy life starts with being
comfortable in your own skin and
appreciating blessing.

Seeing

Look into a person's eyes to understand their
enigmatic personality; as the eyes hold the
light and darkness of their many unspoken
journeys.

Now

Redemption exists in the present moment.

Connected

As time passes, the emotional pains of grief,
fear and anger subside
Only then can the ego liberate these emotions
With fortitude, loves' compassion heals the
heart and mind
Timeless existence provokes a simple gift, the
revelation that happiness and love connects
us all.

I Dreamt of a Woman

Everything is finally possible
There is no wanting for food or pleasure
What happened to that little girl
This child who had so many dreams?
Running bare foot at 13
Collecting soda bottles for a penny candy at
the local grocery store
What happened to that little girl?
What happened to that carefree, simple
confident child?
Sleeping until 10:00 AM
Tea and blueberry muffins, campfires and
marshmallows
What happened to that little girl?
Swimming in the river
Drive-in movies with friends and family
Lying on blankets, watching the clouds float
by
What happened to this simple girl?
This woman and her dreams?

This woman who planned to achieve,
planned to be more, planned to give more
Pleasing more than even she could
anticipate or expect
The child turned into a woman
Followed her dreams
Success happened as she searched for her
Believing in her dreams made it all possible
A little girl left a home
Built on values
Education filled her mind
She learns to follow her heart
Hard working and strong
Falls but gets up
What happened to that little girl?
A strong, kind, intelligent, loving woman
was that little girl's dream
What happened to that little girl?
She achieved her dreams
She loves yourself and all others
Even in sorrows found good
Became kind
Appreciate uniqueness

Original
Learned something new everyday
Smiled
Was always polite
Gave to others
Filled her heart with love and joy
Listen carefully to her intuition
This little girl, became the woman she
dreamed.

About the author

Tammy Lee Clause received her Bachelor of Arts from Marywood University in Scranton, Pennsylvania in 1997. She earned her Jurist Doctorate from Quinnipiac College School of Law in Connecticut in 1990, formerly Bridgeport School of Law. Tammy has been a practicing attorney in Newfoundland, Penna. since December of 1990.

Tammy has found wonderment as she enjoys her pursuits in joyful living surrounded by her family and friends every day and in helping others resolve their legal conflicts with enlightenment. Tammy also loves gardening and cooking.

You can contact Tammy at atyclaus@ptd.net or on her Facebook page at Poetry of Conscious Thought.

May you find your passion and enjoy living your dreams!